Rehoboth:

A Place of Enlargement and Fruitfulness

Discover God's Peace, Provision, and Overflow in your Life

Ruby Evans Leak

Books by Ruby Evans Leak

Loving Yourself From The Inside Out

Unclutter Your Mind:
Transform Your Mind, Renew Your Life

Rehoboth: A Place of Enlargement and Fruitfulness

Contents

Introduction

The Meaning of Rehoboth

The word *Rehoboth* in Hebrew means "broad places" or "room." It is more than just a geographical location; it is a spiritual symbol of God's faithfulness to create space for His people. In Genesis 26:22, Isaac named a well Rehoboth, saying, *"For now the LORD has made room for us, and we shall be fruitful in the land."* This devotional invites all Christians—especially women who carry unique burdens—to discover what it means when God makes room for us.

Rehoboth represents seasons where God shifts us from striving to thriving, from conflict to peace, from lack to overflow. This book will guide you through spiritual reflections, life applications, and prayers to help you step into your own Rehoboth season.

Rehoboth is not just a destination—it is a promise. It is the evidence that after seasons of digging and encountering opposition, God opens up a space uniquely prepared for you. Just as Isaac persevered through contention and strife before reaching Rehoboth, many of us must press through hardship, rejection, and closed doors before arriving at the place God has ordained. Yet the beauty of Rehoboth is this: it assures us that our labor has not been in vain, and that God Himself has established a place of fruitfulness for His children.

For women in particular, who often juggle silent struggles and carry unseen weights, Rehoboth becomes a personal sanctuary. It is the reminder that God sees every tear, every effort, every prayer whispered in the midnight hour. In His perfect timing, He enlarges our territory, makes room for our voices, and settles us into spaces where we can breathe again, heal again, and flourish again.

As you journey through this devotional, may you come to understand that Rehoboth is both an inner reality and an outward blessing. It is God's way of saying, *"I have made room for you. You belong here. You will be fruitful."*

Chapter 1

The Wells of Isaac – A Story of Struggle and Victory

Genesis 26 tells us that Isaac stayed in Gerar during the famine, obeying God's command. The Philistines opposed him, disputing over the wells. He named them Esek (contention) and Sitnah (hostility). Finally, he dug a well without dispute, naming it Rehoboth—symbolizing peace and enlargement.

Struggles often precede fruitfulness. Isaac's journey shows us that contention is not the end—it is preparation. When God finally makes room, no enemy can take it away.

This account reminds us that walking in obedience does not exempt us from trials. Isaac was exactly where God told him to be, yet he still faced opposition and resistance. The presence of struggle does not mean the absence of God—it often means He is shaping us for something greater. Each rejected well, each conflict, and each closed door was building Isaac's perseverance and dependence on the Lord.

Rehoboth represents the shift that happens when God Himself steps in and establishes what man cannot oppose. It is the place of settled peace after relentless striving, the moment when God affirms, *"This is yours, and here you will flourish."* For us today, Rehoboth is more than a physical space—it may be a season of restored relationships, a breakthrough in finances, the healing of a wounded heart, or the opening of a door no one else could unlock.

Like Isaac, we may feel weary from constant battles, but every struggle is evidence that we are digging toward the promise. The enemy may contend, but he cannot cancel what God has ordained. Rehoboth is proof that your waiting, your praying, and your enduring are not wasted. It is the promise that there will come a time when the opposition ceases, and you can finally rest in the spacious place God has prepared for you.

Life Application:

We face our own Esek's and Sitnah's: conflicts at work, family disputes, and financial challenges. Yet God calls us to persevere until we reach our Rehoboth.

Reflection Prompts:

- **Where have you experienced contention or hostility?**

_____

_____

_____

_____

_____

_____

_____

_____

_____

_____

_____

- How has God used struggle to grow your faith?

_____

_____

_____

_____

_____

_____

_____

_____

_____

_____

_____

_____

_____

_____

- **What Rehoboth moment are you believing for?**

_____

_____

_____

_____

_____

_____

_____

_____

_____

_____

_____

_____

_____

_____

_____

_____

Prayer:

Lord, strengthen me to persevere through trials. Lead me from contention into Rehoboth. In Jesus' name, Amen.

Declaration:

I will not quit in the face of struggle. God has made room for me, and I will be fruitful in the land.

Chapter 2

Rehoboth – The Lord Has Made Room

Rehoboth represents God's divine enlargement. It is the space He creates for us to breathe, grow, and flourish. *Ephesians 3:20-21 reminds us that God can do exceedingly, abundantly more than we ask or think.*

Rehoboth is not only about physical expansion, but also spiritual, emotional, and mental enlargement. It is the evidence that God sees our hidden labor and rewards us openly. What once felt cramped, heavy, or filled with opposition becomes a wide-open place of peace. In Rehoboth, you realize that God has not forgotten you, nor has He overlooked the seeds you've sown in tears.

In the story of Isaac, Rehoboth came after seasons of conflict and resistance. Wells were taken from him, but he continued to dig. His persistence was not wasted, because God honored his obedience and faith. The same is true for us—our "digging" through prayer, faithfulness, and endurance leads us to a season where God declares, *"Now I have made room for you."*

When the Lord makes room, it silences the voice of the enemy. It is a testimony that no one can block or steal what God has ordained for your life. Rehoboth is not just a place—it is a shift. It is God's stamp of approval, His divine positioning, and His supernatural provision.

Think about the areas of your life where you have faced closed doors, setbacks, or constant pushbacks. Rehoboth reminds you that those very struggles are often the pathway to enlargement. Every "no" was a redirection. Every delay was preparation. And when the appointed time comes, God will bring you into a spacious place where you can flourish without fear of loss.

Rehoboth also challenges us to embrace the new. The space God makes is not for us to remain stagnant but to expand into new callings, deeper intimacy with Him, and bolder faith. It is a season of stretching, where God enlarges your vision, your capacity to love, and your ability to serve.

Life Application:
Sometimes, closed doors are God's way of directing us toward our Rehoboth. We must trust His timing and not despise small beginnings.

Reflection Prompts:

- **Where in your life do you feel God is making room for you right now?**

_____

_____

_____

_____

_____

_____

_____

_____

- **How have past struggles prepared you for the enlargement God is bringing?**

_____

_____

_____

_____

_____

_____

_____

_____

_____

_____

_____

_____

_____

_____

- **What "new thing" might God be inviting you to step into during your Rehoboth season?**

_____

_____

_____

_____

_____

_____

_____

_____

_____

_____

_____

_____

_____

_____

_____

Prayer:

Lord, I thank You for the promise of Rehoboth. Thank You for making room for me to grow, thrive, and bear fruit. Teach me to trust You when the journey feels hard and to recognize when You are shifting me into a season of enlargement. May I honor You in this new space by walking in faith, humility, and obedience. In Jesus' name, Amen.

Declaration:

This is my season of divine enlargement. God is making room for me, and I will flourish. In Jesus' name, Amen.

Chapter 3

Broad Places – God's Gift of Peace and Provision

Psalm 18:19 declares, "He brought me out into a broad place; He rescued me, because He delighted in me." Rehoboth is that broad place of peace and provision where striving ceases.

The broad place is not just a destination but a spiritual reality. It is the assurance that no matter the storms around you, God has established a safe and spacious place within you. It is where the soul exhales, releasing anxiety, and inhales the calm of God's presence. Just as David declared that God rescued him because He delighted in him, we too can find confidence that God's peace flows from His love for us, not from our circumstances.

In these broad places, God teaches us that provision is not limited to material needs. He supplies wisdom when we are confused, strength when we are weary, hope when we feel defeated, and joy when we are overwhelmed. His provision extends to every corner of our lives—body, soul, and spirit. What once felt like lack is transformed into overflow, not because everything is perfect, but because God's presence fills every gap.

Sometimes the broad place comes after seasons of narrowness—times when life felt suffocating, resources were scarce, or peace seemed far away. But God uses those moments to shape our faith and deepen our trust in Him. When the broad place comes, we value it more because we know what it costs to get there. We learn that true peace is not dependent on perfect circumstances but anchored in God's unchanging faithfulness.

The broad place is also where striving ends. You no longer fight to prove your worth, chase the approval of others, or exhaust yourself trying to control outcomes. Instead, you settle into the rhythm of God's grace, trusting that He will provide, sustain, and enlarge your life in His timing.

Life Application:

Peace is not the absence of problems but the presence of God. When we trust His provision, we find rest even in uncertain seasons. *2 Corinthians 9:8 assures us that God supplies abundantly.*

Reflection Prompts:

- **What does peace look like in your life right now?**

_____

_____

_____

_____

_____

_____

_____

_____

_____

_____

- **In what areas do you need to stop striving and start trusting God's provision?**

_____

_____

_____

_____

_____

_____

_____

_____

_____

_____

_____

_____

_____

_____

- **Where in your life do you need peace right now?**

_____

_____

_____

_____

_____

_____

_____

_____

_____

_____

_____

_____

_____

_____

Prayer:

Lord, I thank You for the broad places You have prepared for me. Even when life feels uncertain, Your peace steadies my heart, and Your provision sustains me. Help me to rest in Your presence, to release my striving, and to trust You in every area of my life. May I always remember that true peace is found not in perfect circumstances but in You alone. In Jesus' name, Amen.

Declaration:

I live in God's broad place. I walk in peace, provision, and freedom.

Chapter 4

Four Types of Blessings at Rehoboth

At Rehoboth, God's blessings manifest in four ways: Spiritual, Material, Undeserved, and Unsolicited. *Deuteronomy 28:2 says blessings will overtake us when we walk in obedience.*

Spiritual Blessings

These are the unseen gifts that sustain us in our walk with Christ—peace that surpasses understanding, joy that cannot be shaken, wisdom for difficult decisions, and strength to endure trials. *Ephesians 1:3 reminds us that we are blessed with every spiritual blessing in the heavenly places in Christ.* At Rehoboth, God enlarges our capacity to know Him deeper, to hear His voice clearly, and to walk in His Spirit with confidence.

Material Blessings

God also provides for our physical needs—resources, finances, shelter, opportunities, and open doors. Material blessings remind us that God cares about every detail of our lives. He is Jehovah Jireh, our Provider. Yet, these blessings are never just for us alone; they are entrusted to us so we can advance the Kingdom, support others in need, and reflect His generosity in the earth.

Undeserved Blessings

These blessings flow purely from grace. We did nothing to earn them, yet God delights in lavishing His love upon us. Times when He spares us from harm, forgives us despite our failures, or answers prayers we barely whispered are examples of His undeserved goodness. They are reminders that His blessings are not a reflection of our perfection, but of His unfailing mercy.

Unsolicited Blessings

These are the blessings that come without warning—overflow that surprises us, favor we didn't ask for, opportunities we didn't see coming, and breakthroughs we couldn't have orchestrated ourselves. *Malachi 3:10 promises that God will open the windows of heaven and pour out blessings we won't have room enough to receive.* Rehoboth is the place where these unexpected blessings overtake us, simply because we are walking in obedience and alignment with God's will.

When we live in awareness of these four types of blessings, we begin to shift from striving to gratitude. We recognize that blessings are not random—they are intentional acts of a loving Father who desires for His children to flourish.

Life Application:

We must recognize and steward each type of blessing—using them to glorify God and bless others.

Reflection Prompts:

- Which type of blessing have you recently experienced most in this season of your life?

_____

_____

_____

_____

_____

_____

_____

_____

_____

_____

_____

_____

_____

_____

- **How can you use your material blessings to glorify God and serve others?**

_____

_____

_____

_____

_____

_____

_____

_____

_____

_____

_____

_____

_____

_____

_____

- When was the last time you paused to thank God for undeserved or unsolicited blessings?

_____

_____

_____

_____

_____

_____

_____

_____

_____

_____

_____

_____

_____

_____

Prayer:

Heavenly Father, thank You for the blessings of Rehoboth. Thank You for spiritual growth, material provision, undeserved grace, and unsolicited favor. Help me to recognize and steward these blessings wisely, that my life may bring glory to Your name and bring good to others. May I never take Your goodness for granted but always walk in gratitude and obedience. In Jesus' name, Amen.

Declaration:

I walk in spiritual, material, undeserved, and unsolicited blessings. God's favor overtakes me.

Chapter 5

From Conflict to Fruitfulness

Conflict often precedes a breakthrough. *Galatians 6:9 encourages us not to grow weary, for in due season we shall reap.*

Seasons of conflict are not wasted seasons. They are often the soil in which God plants the seeds of future fruitfulness. When Isaac faced opposition over the wells in Genesis 26, it was not the end of his story. The contention pushed him forward until he arrived at Rehoboth, the place of enlargement and peace. What looked like a setback was really God's setup for increase.

Conflict teaches us to depend on God more deeply. *James 1:2-4* reminds us to "consider it nothing but joy" when we face trials, because the testing of our faith produces endurance and maturity. The very opposition that wears us down can become the tool God uses to strengthen us.

Fruitfulness is the promise on the other side of conflict. *John 15:5* declares, "I am the vine; you are the branches. Whoever abides in me and I in him, he it is that bears much fruit." When we remain connected to Christ, even seasons of conflict cannot stop the fruit that God has ordained for our lives. In fact, pruning seasons— though painful—prepare us for greater harvests.

Conflict also refines our character. *Romans 5:3-5* says, "We rejoice in our sufferings, knowing that suffering produces endurance, and endurance produces character, and character produces hope." Fruitfulness is not just about external blessings, but about an inner transformation where our hearts, attitudes, and faith grow stronger.

It is important to remember that conflict is temporary, but God's promise of fruitfulness is eternal. *Psalm 126:5-6* declares, "Those who sow in tears shall reap with shouts of joy! He who goes out weeping, bearing the seed for sowing, shall come home with shouts of joy, bringing his sheaves with him." The tears you cry in conflict are watering the ground of your harvest.

When we hold firm in obedience, even in the face of opposition, we position ourselves to step into a season where God Himself brings the increase. Conflict cannot cancel your calling, delay cannot deny your destiny, and opposition cannot override God's ordained fruitfulness for your life.

Life Application:

Like Isaac, we must keep moving until we find our Rehoboth. Fruitfulness comes after faithfulness.

Reflection Prompts:

- What conflict are you currently facing that may be preparing you for greater fruitfulness?

_____

_____

_____

_____

_____

_____

_____

_____

_____

_____

_____

_____

_____

- **How has God used past struggles to shape your character and strengthen your faith?**

_____

_____

_____

_____

_____

_____

_____

_____

_____

_____

_____

_____

_____

_____

- **What promises of God have you held onto in a season of conflict?**

_____

_____

_____

_____

_____

_____

_____

_____

_____

_____

_____

_____

_____

_____

Prayer

Father, I thank You that conflict is not the end of my story. Thank You for the reminder that in due season, I will reap if I do not give up. Strengthen me to endure, refine me in the process, and bring me into the fruitfulness You have promised. Help me to see conflict as preparation, not punishment, and to trust You in every season. In Jesus' name, Amen.

Declaration:

My season of conflict is producing fruit. I will reap because I will not faint.

Chapter 6

Rehoboth in Our Modern Walk with God

Rehoboth is not just Isaac's story—it is ours. Today, God still makes room in our families, careers, ministries, and hearts.

In a world filled with competition, chaos, and constant striving, the promise of Rehoboth reminds us that God is still the One who enlarges our steps and establishes our paths. *Proverbs 18:16* declares, "A man's gift makes room for him and brings him before the great." When God makes room, He opens doors that no man can shut (*Revelation 3:8*), and He positions us exactly where He desires us to be.

Rehoboth in our modern walk may look like reconciliation in a broken family, peace in the middle of a financial storm, or clarity when making a career decision. It may be a ministry opportunity that you didn't seek out but that God entrusted to you. In every case, it is the Lord reminding us that He delights in creating space for His children to thrive.

Walking into Rehoboth requires faith and obedience. *Isaiah 43:19* declares, "See, I am doing a new thing! Now it springs up; do you not perceive it? I am making a way in the wilderness and streams in the wasteland." Just as Isaac had to keep digging wells even after contention and opposition, we too must continue to trust, believe, and act on God's promises even when doors seem to close in our faces.

In our modern lives, Rehoboth also calls us to stewardship. The room God creates is not simply for our comfort, but for His glory. *Matthew 5:16* reminds us, "Let your light so shine before men, that they may see your good works and glorify your Father in heaven." Whether in our homes, workplaces, or ministries, the enlargement God provides is meant to influence others for Christ.

Rehoboth is also a place of rest. *Matthew 11:28-29* says, "Come to me, all you who are weary and burdened, and I will give you rest. Take my yoke upon you and learn from me… and you will find rest for your souls." In the midst of life's pressures, God's Rehoboth reminds us that we do not have to strive in our own strength—His presence provides peace, and His Spirit equips us to flourish.

Life Application:
Whether it is a new job, restored relationship, or inner healing, Rehoboth is where God's promises become reality.

Reflection Prompts:

- **What area of your life do you need to surrender so that God can bring you into your Rehoboth?**

_____

_____

_____

_____

_____

_____

_____

_____

- **How will you honor Him when He does?**

_____

_____

_____

_____

_____

_____

_____

_____

_____

_____

_____

_____

_____

_____

Prayer

Lord, thank You for reminding me that Rehoboth is not just Isaac's testimony but mine as well. Help me to see where You are making room in my life and give me the courage to step into those places with faith and obedience. May I steward every blessing, every opportunity, and every open door for Your glory. In Jesus' name, Amen.

Declaration:

I am walking in my Rehoboth. God is making room for me today.

Chapter 7

Living in the Overflow

Rehoboth leads us to overflow. *Psalm 23:5 says, "My cup overflows."* Overflow is not just for survival but for generosity and kingdom impact.

The overflow of God is a sign of His abundant nature. He never blesses sparingly—He pours until there is more than enough. *John 10:10* reminds us that Jesus came so that we may have life and have it more abundantly. When God makes room, He doesn't just give us space to exist; He fills that space with blessings that ripple outward to others.

Living in the overflow means recognizing that what God provides is not solely for us, but also through us. *2 Corinthians 9:11* declares, "You will be enriched in every way so that you can be generous on every occasion, and through us your generosity will result in thanksgiving to God." In other words, God enlarges our lives so that our blessings become a testimony and resource for others.

Overflow is also connected to faithfulness. When we remain obedient and faithful in small things, God positions us for greater outpouring. *Luke 16:10* says, "Whoever can be trusted with very little can also be trusted with much." Isaac's persistence through conflict led him not only to peace but to fruitfulness and abundance at Rehoboth.

This kind of overflow is not limited to material wealth. It includes peace that spills into every conversation, joy that radiates even in trials, wisdom that blesses those around us, and love that draws others closer to Christ. *Romans 15:13* captures this beautifully: "May the God of hope fill you with all joy and peace as you trust in him, so that you may overflow with hope by the power of the Holy Spirit."

Living in the overflow requires a heart posture of stewardship and gratitude. God blesses us so that we may pour into others, whether that's mentoring, giving, serving, or encouraging. It is a cycle of divine generosity: as God pours into us, we pour into others, and He continues to pour back into us. *Malachi 3:10* reminds us that God promises to "open the windows of heaven and pour out a blessing until it overflows" when we walk in obedience.

Biblical Example: The Widow's Oil

One of the clearest pictures of overflow is found in *2 Kings 4:1–7*. A widow cried out to the prophet Elisha because her creditors were coming to take her sons as slaves. All she had was a small jar of oil. Elisha told her to gather as many empty vessels as she could, shut the door, and pour the oil into them. As she poured, the oil kept flowing until every vessel was full. When she returned to Elisha, he told her to sell the oil, pay her debts, and live on the rest.

This story shows us that God takes what looks like "not enough" and turns it into more than enough. The miracle of the oil was not just about survival—it was about provision that restored her dignity, freed her family from bondage, and sustained her future. That is the essence of overflow: God meets our needs and then goes beyond them, so that we may walk in freedom and abundance.

The widow's obedience and faith activated the miracle. Likewise, our willingness to trust God, even with the little we have, creates space for Him to multiply it into overflow.

Life Application:
God blesses us so we can bless others. Overflow is meant to be shared.

Reflection Prompts:

- **What "small jar of oil" do you have that God may want to multiply?**

_____

_____

_____

_____

_____

_____

_____

_____

_____

_____

- Are you making room in your life—like the widow's empty vessels—for God's overflow?

_____

_____

_____

_____

_____

_____

_____

_____

_____

_____

_____

_____

_____

_____

- **How can you share your overflow to release others from bondage or lack?**

_____

_____

_____

_____

_____

_____

_____

_____

_____

_____

_____

_____

_____

_____

Prayer

Lord, I thank You for being the God of overflow. Just as You multiplied the widow's oil, I believe You can take what seems small in my life and expand it for Your glory. Help me to walk in faith and obedience, making room for Your abundance. May my overflow not only meet my needs but also impact others, breaking chains, bringing freedom, and revealing Your goodness. In Jesus' name, Amen.

Declaration:

I live in overflow. My blessings spill over to others.

Chapter 8

The Rehoboth Life –
Walking in
Enlargement and
Multiplication

Rehoboth is not a one-time event but a lifestyle. God continually enlarges our capacity when we walk in faith. *Deuteronomy 6:12 reminds us not to forget Him when we prosper.*

Living the Rehoboth life means understanding that enlargement is not just about personal blessings, but about kingdom purpose. When God makes room for us, it is so His glory may be revealed through our lives. *Isaiah 54:2-3* declares, "Enlarge the place of your tent, stretch your tent curtains wide, do not hold back; lengthen your cords, strengthen your stakes. For you will spread out to the right and to the left; your descendants will dispossess nations and settle in their desolate cities." Enlargement is always tied to multiplication—it is God's way of extending His promises through us.

The Rehoboth life also requires humility and stewardship. *Luke 12:48* reminds us, "To whom much is given, much will be required." When God expands our territory, we must manage it wisely, remembering that prosperity without purpose can lead to pride. Instead, God calls us to use our enlargement to serve, to give, and to influence others for Christ.

Walking in enlargement means walking in faith, because multiplication often begins with small steps of obedience. *Zechariah 4:10* encourages us not to despise small beginnings, for the Lord rejoices to see the work begin. Just as Isaac kept digging wells until he reached Rehoboth, we must persist in faith, trusting that every step of obedience prepares us for greater capacity.

Multiplication is a promise of Rehoboth life. *John 15:8* says, "This is to my Father's glory, that you bear much fruit, showing yourselves to be my disciples." God doesn't just want us to survive—He wants us to thrive, to bear fruit, and to multiply. Whether in our families, our careers, or our ministries, His desire is that we become vessels through which His abundance flows.

The Rehoboth life is also a life of continual remembrance. We must guard against forgetting the Source of our enlargement. *Deuteronomy 8:18* reminds us, "But remember the Lord your God, for it is he who gives you the ability to produce wealth and so confirms his covenant." Every breakthrough, every opportunity, and every blessing is a reminder that we stand where we are because of His hand, not our own.

Finally, walking in enlargement calls us to a legacy mindset. God's multiplication is generational—what He begins in us, He desires to flow through us to our children, our communities, and even nations. *Psalm 115:14-15* declares, "May the Lord cause you to flourish, both you and your children. May you be blessed by the Lord, the Maker of heaven and earth." Rehoboth is not just for today—it is the beginning of blessings that ripple into eternity.

Biblical Example: Jabez's Prayer for Enlargement
One powerful example of the Rehoboth life is found in *1 Chronicles 4:10.* Jabez cried out to God, saying, "Oh, that You would bless me indeed and enlarge my

territory! Let Your hand be with me and keep me from harm so that I will be free from pain." Scripture tells us that God granted his request.

Jabez's prayer was simple yet bold. He recognized that true enlargement comes only from God's hand. His request was not just for material gain, but for God's presence, protection, and purpose in his life. Jabez lived the Rehoboth life by daring to ask God for more, and by trusting Him to provide it. His example reminds us that enlargement begins with prayer and faith, and it results in living a life that impacts others for generations.

Relating Rehoboth to Our Lives Today

For us, living the Rehoboth life might look like:

- A single mother who struggled to make ends meet suddenly finds doors opening for a new job with better pay and flexible hours. That is her Rehoboth.

- A young man battling discouragement in his career is offered an opportunity that aligns with his gifts and passions. That's God enlarging his territory.

- A woman who carried years of shame and hurt discovers freedom and healing through Christ and begins mentoring others with similar struggles. That is multiplication in action.

- A family that once faced constant conflict experiences reconciliation, laughter, and love flowing again at their dinner table. That's walking in the broad place of God's peace.

Your Rehoboth life might not always look like material success. Sometimes it's the peace in your mind when anxiety used to control you, the restoration of your joy after a season of grief, or the courage to step into a new chapter you never thought possible.

Life Application:

Living the Rehoboth life means choosing faith, gratitude, and stewardship daily.

Reflection Prompts:

- In what areas of your life do you see God enlarging your capacity right now?

_____

_____

_____

_____

_____

_____

_____

_____

_____

_____

_____

_____

_____

- How can you steward the multiplication He is bringing so that it glorifies Him?

_____

_____

_____

_____

_____

_____

_____

_____

_____

_____

_____

_____

_____

_____

- **Like Jabez, are you bold enough to pray for God to enlarge your territory?**

_____

_____

_____

_____

_____

_____

_____

_____

_____

_____

_____

_____

_____

_____

- **Which of the everyday examples above feels most relatable to your own Rehoboth journey?**

_____

_____

_____

_____

_____

_____

_____

_____

_____

_____

_____

_____

_____

Prayer

Father, thank You for the gift of Rehoboth—not just as a moment, but as a lifestyle of enlargement and multiplication. Help me to walk in humility, steward Your blessings well, and always remember that every increase comes from You. Like Jabez, I ask You to enlarge my territory, let Your hand be with me, and keep me from harm. May my life bear much fruit and create a legacy of faith, generosity, and obedience that impacts generations to come. In Jesus' name, Amen.

Declaration:

I live the Rehoboth life. God is enlarging me daily, and I will not forget Him.

Conclusion

Embracing the Rehoboth Life

Rehoboth is more than a well Isaac dug—it is a promise of God's faithfulness. It is the wide, open space where God makes room for His children to thrive. Through contention, hostility, and struggle, we learn perseverance. Through Rehoboth, we experience peace, provision, overflow, and multiplication.

This devotional journey has shown us that God is still leading His people into broad places. Whether you are waiting for your Rehoboth or already living in it, remember that God's promises are true. He is the same yesterday, today, and forever.

Hebrews 13:8 declares, "Jesus Christ is the same yesterday and today and forever." Just as He was faithful to Isaac, He will be faithful to you. When the journey feels long and the opposition fierce, hold on to the assurance of *Habakkuk 2:3*: "For the vision is yet for an appointed time; though it tarry, wait for it; because it will surely come, it will not tarry." Rehoboth may not come overnight, but it is certain in God's perfect timing.

Rehoboth is also a reminder to live with expectation. *Ephesians 3:20* promises that God "is able to do exceedingly abundantly above all that we ask or think, according to the power that works in us." When you step into your Rehoboth, it is not the end of your journey but the beginning of a greater walk with God. He enlarges your territory so you can bless others and reflect His glory.

Finally, embracing the Rehoboth life requires gratitude and trust. *1 Thessalonians 5:16–18* urges us to "Rejoice always, pray continually, give thanks in all circumstances; for this is God's will for you in Christ Jesus." Gratitude keeps our hearts tender, while trust keeps us anchored in God's unshakable faithfulness.

As you close this devotional, may you hold fast to the truth of *Psalm 37:4-5*: "Delight yourself in the Lord, and he will give you the desires of your heart. Commit your way to the Lord; trust in him, and he will act." Your Rehoboth is secure in His hands.

Closing Prayer

Heavenly Father, I thank You for the journey of Rehoboth. Thank You for teaching me through seasons of conflict, perseverance, and waiting that You are faithful to bring me into broad places. I receive Your peace, provision, overflow, and multiplication as promises for my life.

Lord, help me to walk daily in the Rehoboth life—with gratitude in my heart, trust in Your timing, and faith in Your unfailing love. May I never forget that every open door and every blessing come from You alone. Use my Rehoboth to bless others, to glorify Your name, and to leave a legacy of faith for generations to come.

I declare today, by faith, that You have made room for me—and in this space, I will thrive. In Jesus' name, Amen.

Daily Declaration

"I am living in my Rehoboth. God has made room for me, and I will be fruitful in the land. I walk in peace, provision, overflow, and multiplication. I will not forget the Lord in my prosperity, and I will use my blessings to glorify Him and bless others. My life is a testimony of His faithfulness, and I am stepping boldly into the broad places He has prepared for me."

Bibliography

- The Holy Bible, Amplified Bible (AMP)

- The Holy Bible, New Living Translation (NLT)

- The Holy Bible, King James Version (KJV)

- Commentaries on Genesis 26

- Vine's Expository Dictionary of Biblical Words

- Strong's Concordance (Hebrew word study for Rehoboth)

About the Author

Ruby Evans Leak is a transformational life coach, author, and inspirational speaker who empowers women to live whole and fruitful lives. As the Founder and Executive Director of **Evolve Tranzishenz Houz Inc.**, Ruby provides housing and supportive services for women returning to society. She is also the visionary behind the **GrandLade™ Brand**, which uplifts grandparents raising grandchildren.

Her mission is simple yet powerful: to remind every believer that *God will make room for you. Learn more at https://linktr.ee/rubyevansleak*